ALL NEW
BEAUTIF
BRAIDS

Hair Designer
MARY BETH JANSSEN-FLEISCHMAN

Contributing Writer
JUDY RAMBERT

PUBLICATIONS INTERNATIONAL, LTD.

CONTENTS

Louis Weber, C.E.O.
Publications International, Ltd.
7373 North Cicero Avenue
Lincolnwood, Illinois 60646

Front cover, clockwise from top left: Sculptured Pattern (page 17), Modern Glamour (page 39), Ingenue (page 61), and Sleek and Festive (page 31).
Back cover: Romantic Textures (page 14).

Photographer
Irena Lukasiewicz

Models
Suzanne Favors/The Models Workshop Studio
Laurie White/Royal Model Management
Raheda Shurn/Royal Model Management
Amanda Sassano/Royal Model Management

Makeup artist
Karen Lynn

Hair Designer **Mary Beth Janssen-Fleischman** is International Artistic Director for Pivot Point International, Inc. and Artistic Director for *Design Forum*. Mary Beth was hair designer for the first book in this series, *Beautiful Braids*.

Contributing Writer **Judy Rambert** is Vice President of Education for Pivot Point International, Inc. Judy was contributing writer for the first book in this series, *Beautiful Braids*.

INTRODUCTION

Even with designer clothing, perfectly applied makeup, and fine jewelry, no look is really complete without a distinctive hairstyle to top it off. Unique and striking hair designs have been a part of the fashion world throughout history, and braiding has consistently been one of the most effective ways to design individual styles. By combining various braid techniques and applying them in different ways, you can create a whole range of statements, from sophisticated and elegant to carefree and casual. You can develop styles that work well for the young or old, that are suitable for any occasion, that match a particular mood or outfit, or that are just plain fun to do. You can give yourself a whole new look any time you want, and perhaps best of all, you can change the way you look tomorrow if you decide you don't like it.

Once you master some of the basic techniques in this book, you can create many of your own designs at home. As in any art form, the more you practice the better you become. The designs featured in this book have been created by a very skilled professional, so don't be discouraged if your first results are not an exact duplicate. Our intent is to show you some classic techniques that you can use on yourself, your friends, or your family between professional salon visits. So have some fun, experiment with the designs we feature, and create some of your own.

A note about the instructions in this book: To avoid confusion, we have used the terms "left" and "right" to refer to the *reader's* left and right.

  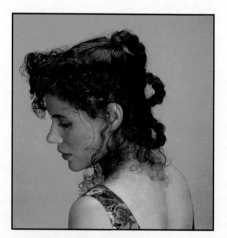

TECHNIQUES

BRAIDS

Two basic techniques create three-strand braided designs. One is **overbraiding,** and the other is **underbraiding.** In overbraiding, the outside strands are crossed over the center strand. In underbraiding, the outside strands are crossed under the center strand. Braids created with an overbraid technique have also been called English braids; those with an underbraid technique have been called Dutch braids. The choice between overbraiding or underbraiding depends upon your personal preference and which technique is more comfortable for you to perform.

When these two techniques are performed on free-hanging ponytails, there is only a slight difference in the braided pattern. The visible difference occurs when these techniques are combined with the addition of new sections of hair gathered from the scalp and added to the outside strands while you continue to braid. Overbraiding with added sections, which is also known as a French braid, produces a flat or **inverted braid** pattern. When you incorporate new sections of hair while underbraiding, the result will be a raised or **projected braid.** This technique creates corn-row designs, along with many other styles.

We have also incorporated a **four-strand round braid** into some of these designs. This technique makes an unusual-looking chainlike braid, and it's not difficult to master. The outside strands are brought under two strands and back over one.

TWO-STRAND OVERLAP

This technique features only two strands, which are alternately crossed from one side to the other side. The technique can be performed on the free ends of a ponytail or along the scalp with new sections added. The result is a beautiful herringbone pattern, which has also been called a fish tail.

TWISTS

The other technique featured in the book is twisting. Individual strands can be twisted independently, or two strands can be twisted together. The resulting pattern resembles a rope. This technique can be performed on the free ends of a ponytail, or the twist can be combined with new additions picked up along the hairline that are incorporated into the twist.

Inverted Overbraid

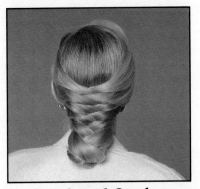
Projected Underbraid

Two-Strand Overlap

Single-Strand Twists

To help you get started and to make it easier to learn the designs included in this book, try these suggestions and "inside tips" from the professionals.

PRODUCTS

Pomade

Use a pomade to remove static, control flyaway ends, and add a glossy sheen to either straight or curly hair. Pomade should be used sparingly, though. Apply a very small amount to one hand and liquefy it between your palms. Then run your hands through the hair before braiding or use it for small touch-ups afterward.

Gel

Gel will control hair lengths too, but it produces more of a wet effect than pomade does. You can apply gel to all of the hair before you braid, or, when you want a clean, off-the-face effect, you can apply it to the perimeter hairline where lengths tend to be shorter.

Gel can also be used after a braid is finished to smooth down loose or uncontrolled hairs. Apply it to your fingertip or to the end of a hairpin; then direct it on top of the stray hairs to encourage them back into the braided pattern.

Hair Spray

Besides using hair spray to hold the finished design in place, try using it in spot areas as you work. Also, if you want to create a soft finish but need to control the hair, spray lightly into the palm of your hand and then smooth over the surface of the hair to control flyaway strands before you braid.

BEADED FINISH

When selecting beads, consider their color and weight and the amount of light they reflect. Glass reflects the most light; plastic and wood weigh the least. Avoid putting heavy beads on fragile hair.

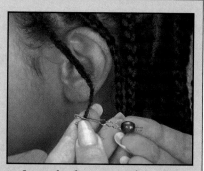

1. Begin by squeezing the closed end of a hairpin to make it smaller. Then place the end of the braid between the open ends of the hairpin.

2. Insert both prongs of the hairpin through the hole in the bead.

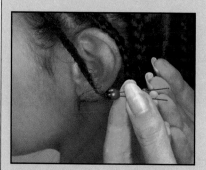

3. Thread the bead onto the braid by pulling the pin through the bead.

4. Move the bead along the length of the braid, positioning it where it looks best.

5. The bead should fit snugly, so if the opening is too large, you may need either to move the bead higher up the braid or choose another bead.

Coated Bands

Ordinary rubber bands can place undue tension on the hair, which may cause hair breakage. Using a coated rubber band to secure ponytails and the ends of a braid will reduce the stress on the hair. This extra consideration will help keep your hair in better condition.

ACCESSORIES

Adding an ornament, barrette, ribbon, or any of the wide assortment of accessories available can finish your completed design. The selection is based on practical purposes—to keep ends secure—as well as decorative options. Both the occasion and your wardrobe should influence the type of accessory you select and the way that you work it into the hairstyle.

For business, simplicity is generally the key. For active sports, choose barrettes, grips, or ribbons that adhere with tension. For special occasions, pearls or silver and gold ornaments give extra elegance and sophistication. Don't forget a great standby—flowers, either fresh or silk. From large dahlias to smaller baby's breath, flowers pinned into the design can add a touch of romantic femininity.

Remember, not every design requires accessorizing; sometimes the pattern in the hair is enough. If you do choose ornamentation, make sure that it matches the feeling that you want to portray.

Your professional salon, as well as hobby craft stores, fabric stores, and millinery sections of department stores, can all be resources for you to find the right accessory to add the final touch to your design for long hair.

SPIRAL WRAPPING

By wrapping a cord or ribbon in a spiral fashion around the braid ends, you can cover a band or even eliminate it entirely.

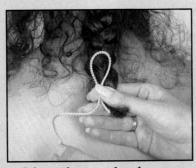

1. Select a long cord, at least ten or twelve inches in length. Loop one end and hold it next to the ends of the hair.

2. Wrap the loose end around the hair from the bottom upward.

3. When you get toward the top and enough of the loop is still showing, insert the end of the cord through the loop.

4. Hold the hair end as shown and pull slowly on the bottom end of the cord until the loop disappears inside the wrapped area. Clip off the extra cord ends on the top and bottom.

5. The result looks more difficult then it really is. Vary the effect by using different types of cord or ribbon to complement your wardrobe or reflect the mood of the finished design.

CHARMINGLY CHIC
DRAPED OVERBRAID

This design requires hair long enough to reach at least halfway down the back. The lengths are gathered at the top of the head and braided; the braid is then draped down the center back of the head. It's surprisingly easy to do on your own hair. Here we've used the overbraid technique, but you can also use an underbraid. We've braided the hair when dry, which causes a slight drape in the hair around the face. If you braid the hair while it is wet, the hair will remain very close to the head.

1. Comb all the hair smoothly upward to the top of the head. If necessary to control stray strands, mist the hairline with water or hair spray.

2. Divide the hair into three equal-size sections.

3. Cross the left strand over the center strand. The center strand moves to the left and the left strand now becomes the center strand.

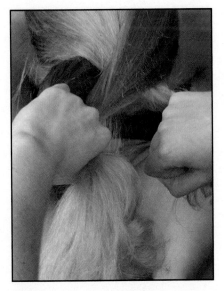

4. Reach over and grasp the right strand. Direct it over the center strand. The right strand now becomes the center strand.

5. Repeat the procedure by continuing to cross the side strands over the center strands, alternating left and right. Keep the head bent down to make braiding easier.

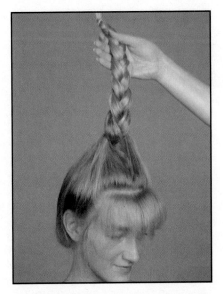

6. Overbraid down the length of the hair and secure the ends with a band. Lift the braid straight upward, allowing shorter fringe lengths to fall down naturally. These lengths can be left straight or curled with a curling iron later.

(continued)

7. Pin behind the base of the braid with bobby pins to secure the hair upward.

8. Fold the braid over the pins and drape it down the center of the head.

9. Choose ornamentation to match the occasion and the colors being worn. For a casual look, secure a barrette or small bow to the end of the braid.

10. For a more formal version, try an ornamental elastic holder. The hole in this ornament allows you to insert the end of the braid into the holder.

11. Secure the end of the hair with a bobby pin to position both the braid and the ornament. Pin around the ornament in several places.

12. Shorter fringe lengths around the face can be incorporated casually by releasing them and curling them with a curling iron for a soft finish.

SLEEK AND MODERN
FIGURE-EIGHT OVERBRAID

This classic look is suitable for either business or evening wear. The pattern at the top of the head is composed of two braids arranged like a figure eight. Here we've positioned the two braids so that the figure eight is horizontal, but you can also create a vertical design. The size and shape of the figure eight will depend upon how long the hair is and how far apart you place the ponytails before they are braided.

The smooth, interesting front of the design is achieved by leaving side panels of hair out of the braids and then directing these panels across the top of the head in an overlap pattern.

11

1. Section off an area of hair on each side of the head with curved partings and secure each section with a clip. Brush the remaining hair smooth and form it into two ponytails side by side at the top of the head.

2. Notice that the front hairline between the curved partings is included in the ponytails.

3. Braid each ponytail using the overbraid technique. Begin by dividing one of the ponytails into three equal-size strands.

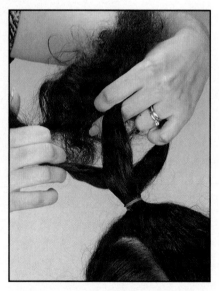

4. Reach across to grasp the right strand with your thumb and forefinger.

5. Cross this right strand over the center strand so that the right strand is now the center strand.

6. Reach across to the left side and grasp the left strand. Cross it over the center strand so that it is in the center position. Continue overbraiding down the length of the ponytail, crossing the outside strands over the center strand. Secure the ends with a coated band.

7. Overbraid the other ponytail in the same way. Secure the ends with a coated band.

8. Unclip the left side section and comb it smoothly upward, directing it over the top and around the braid on the right.

9. Curve the end around the base of the braid and pin with hairpins to secure it.

10. Unclip the right side and direct it over the top of the head. Wrap the end around the base of the braid on the left and secure it with hairpins.

11. The figure eight is created last. Curve the right braid back to form a loop and then forward around the base of the braid on the opposite side. Pin the end of the right braid to the base of the opposite braid.

12. Repeat Step 11 for the left braid. You can experiment by creating different shapes, depending on the length of the braids.

ROMANTIC TEXTURES
TRIPLE OVERBRAID

Three inverted braids are featured in this design. They are formed with the standard overbraid technique, but new sections of hair are added as you move down the braid. All three braids are joined at the center back and contribute to one final, larger braid. The hair lengths around the hairline can be left free to frame the face, as we've done here, or all the hair can be included in the braids. You can do this design on either damp hair or dry hair. Damp hair will produce a graphic design closer to the head, whereas dry hair will tend to look fuller or softer.

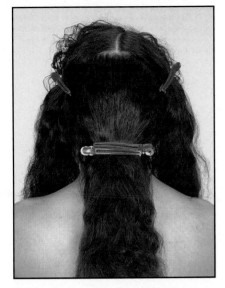

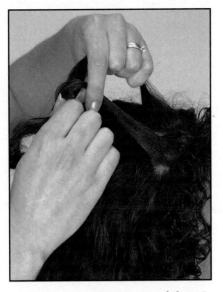

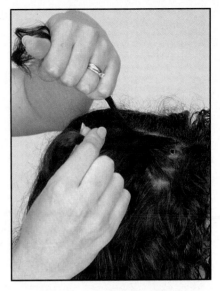

1. Let the lengths of hair framing the face along the hairline fall free; separate them with a free-form, zigzag parting. Section the remaining hair into three areas. Here we have divided the sides with a center part and sectioned off the back with a parting from one ear to the other.

2. Begin to overbraid one of the side areas of hair. Separate a triangular section of hair at the front of the area and divide it into three equal-size strands. Reach across to grasp the right strand. Cross it over the center strand, moving the right strand into the center position.

3. Grasp the left strand and cross it over the center strand so that the left strand moves into the center position.

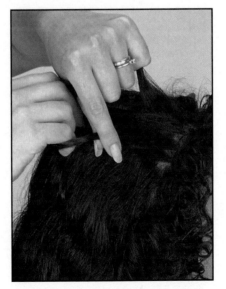

4. Pick up a section of hair from the area between the zigzag parting made in Step 1 and the braided area.

5. Reach across with your thumb and forefinger to grasp the new picked-up section along with the outside strand.

6. Cross this new, combined strand over the center strand.

7. Pick up a section of similar size on the left, from the area between the center part and the braided area. Join it with the left strand and cross the combined strand over the center strand.

8. Continue braiding down the center of the area. Pick up new sections of hair from both sides, combine them with the outside strands, and cross them over the center.

9. Once you have picked up all the hair in the side area, continue overbraiding down the remaining lengths of hair. Clip the end of the braid to hold it temporarily.

10. Repeat Steps 2 through 9 on the other side, balancing the position of the braid with the one on the first side. Then overbraid the back area, adding sections as you go along, until you reach the location where you want the three braids to connect.

11. Create three strands using all of the braided hair. For the first strand, add the left strand from the center back braid to all three strands of the left braid. The center strand of the center back braid is the second strand. The third strand consists of the right strand from the center back braid and all three strands of the right side braid.

12. Continue the braid by crossing the combined left strand over the center strand. Consistent tension is very important during this process. Continue overbraiding down the length of the strand. Secure the ends with a coated or decorated band. To spiral-wrap the ends with gold cord, see the directions on page 7.

SCULPTURED PATTERN
PROJECTED UNDERBRAID

This design uses the basic underbraid technique but adds new sections of hair to the outside strands as you braid. The outside strands are always crossed under the center, which causes the braided pattern to project upward. Our version curves a single braid asymmetrically down the back from the right side to the left and back. The same technique can be used to create a braid that moves directly down the center back.

SCULPTURED PATTERN

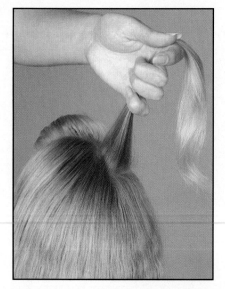

1. Begin at the front hairline slightly off to one side. Create a triangular section of hair. Any short lengths at the forehead can be left free.

2. Divide the section into three equal-size strands. Anchor the right strand, reach under the center strand, and grasp the left strand. Keep your fingers close to the head and, if necessary, rest your hands on the head.

3. Direct the left strand under the center strand so that the left strand moves into the center position.

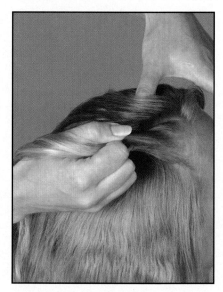

4. With your left hand, reach under the center and grasp the right strand.

5. Cross the right strand under the center strand. The right strand has now exchanged positions with the center strand.

6. Anchor all three strands with your right hand, keeping them separate. With your left thumb, pick up hair from the scalp along the left side.

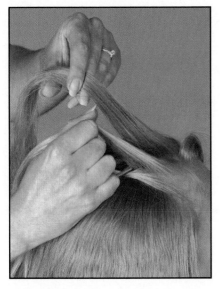

7. Combine this newly picked-up hair with the left strand. Smooth the length of the strand to untangle the hair.

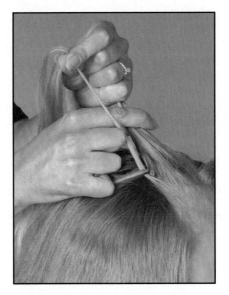

8. Reach under the center strand with your right hand to grasp the new combined strand and pull it under the center strand.

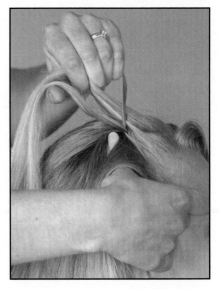

9. Transfer all three strands to the left, keeping them separate. Use your right thumb to part through and pick up hair on the right side from the hairline to the braid.

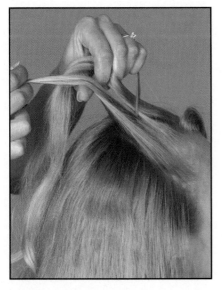

10. Join this picked-up hair with the right strand. Run your hand down the length of the hair to smooth and untangle the hair.

11. Reach under the center strand with your left hand and grasp the new combined strand. Direct it to the center position.

12. Continue underbraiding, picking up hair from either side and combining it with the outside strand. Direct the braid toward the center back of the head.

(continued)

13. When you reach the back of the head, start to direct the braid back toward the right again. This will create a gentle curve in the braided pattern. Run your hand through the strands as necessary to keep the strands smooth and tangle-free.

14. Keep your hands close to the head as you braid and keep the head in a forward position to maintain tension. Continue to pick up sections on either side of the braid until all the hair has been incorporated.

15. Once all the hair has been picked up, continue the underbraiding technique down the length of the hair.

16. Secure the ends by wrapping a band several times around them. The finished braid moves in a slight curve from the right side to the left and back again. You may want to control ends that pop out from the braid by applying a small amount of gel.

17. You can create another look by wrapping the free end of the braid into a chignon. Curve the free end of the braid around into a circle. Use hairpins along the edges to secure the chignon and pin it into position.

18. You can create a larger curved shape by directing the braid upward and forming a large circle. If the hair is not long enough to fill a larger curve, you can balance the sparse areas with an ornament. Here, peacock feathers inserted into the braid camouflage the ends and fill in the circle.

EXOTICA
MULTIPLE UNDERBRAIDS

This basic design, often called "corn-rows," consists of many narrow underbraids positioned along the scalp. A variety of patterns can be formed. This particular pattern begins with vertical braids in the lower back of the head. To design the braids on the top part of the head, a single braid is positioned off-center from the front hairline to the completed back section. The remaining braids radiate from the front of this braid to the lower back.

1. Isolate the lower back section of hair by securing the top and side lengths out of your way. Subdivide this section into vertical panels. You will be braiding each panel using a three-strand underbraid technique.

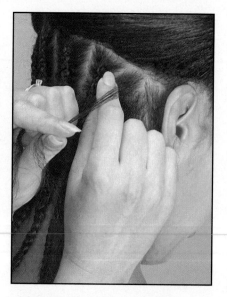

2. Divide one section into three equal-size strands. With your right hand, reach under the center strand, grasp the left strand, and cross it under the center strand. The left strand is now in the center position.

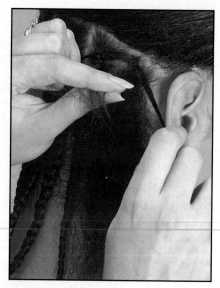

3. Now reach under the center strand with your left hand, grasp the right strand, and direct it into the center position.

4. Use your thumb and forefinger to pick up hair from the right half of the section. Join this picked-up hair to the right strand and bring it under the center. Continue adding hair from along the scalp as you braid.

5. Maintain tension on the braid by keeping your hands close to the head. Duplicating the hand position shown makes this easy to do.

6. To keep the braid centered within the panel, try to pick up the same amount of hair on each side of the braid.

7. After you have picked up all the hair from the scalp, continue to underbraid the free ends. An easy way to do these tiny braids is first to grasp the center with your thumb and forefinger and secure the outside strand between your little finger and ring finger.

8. Then turn your palm upward. This automatically swings the outside strand, which is secured by your little finger, under and into the center. Then grasp this new center strand with the opposite hand and turn the hand upward. Repeat the procedure to the end.

9. You can secure the ends in many ways. Here they have been sewn with a decorative thread. To do this, thread the needle and knot the two ends together. Wrap the thread around the hair ends and insert the needle through the loop of the thread.

10. Pull to tighten the thread around the hair.

11. Sew through the loop several times. Repeat until the ends are secure.

12. Clean partings between the braids are important not only to the looks of the design but also for personal comfort. Stray hairs braided into the wrong section can hurt. They can cause breakage, too, if the tension on the hair is great.

(continued)

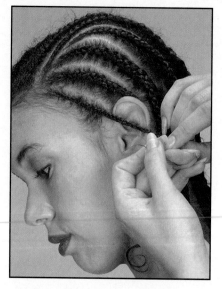

13. Now start to braid the top area. Create a narrow section from the front hairline to the just-completed braided area as shown. Keep the remaining unbraided lengths secured and out of your way. Position this section so that the braid falls in between the lower back partings.

14. Once the first top braid is completed, create a new panel next to it, following the curve of the head. Part carefully and cleanly. Braid that panel and finish the ends. Continue parting new panels, following the curve of the head, and braiding them. The last panel will be parallel to the hairline.

15. Secure the ends of the braids with threads as each braid is finished. Notice how the panels curve with the shape of the head.

16. The top braids fall between the lower braids, forming a pleasing design.

17. Now return to the front and create braids that radiate from the top down on the opposite side. Part cleanly and keep the unbraided hair secured and out of the way. Shorter lengths at the hairline can be left free.

18. Once all the braids are completed, you can curl the ends slightly with a curling iron to create a clean finish.

FUTURISTIC FLAIR
LOOPED UNDERBRAIDS

In this design, the ends of one braid are joined to the beginning strands of another braid. This makes the first braid stand out in a loop. Here we've used three loops. You can make smaller loops by increasing the number of braids. Strands casually released around the hairline create a soft, romantic expression. If your hair isn't naturally curly, you can use a curling iron on these face-framing strands.

1. Divide and clip the hair into three sections—top, middle, and bottom. Allow the lengths around the hairline to frame the face freely. Here we used a free-form zigzag parting line.

2. The top section will form the first braid. Divide it into three equal-size strands. Reach under the center strand to grasp the right strand with your thumb and forefinger. Direct it under the center strand and into the center position.

3. Now reach under and grasp the strand on the left. Direct it under the center strand.

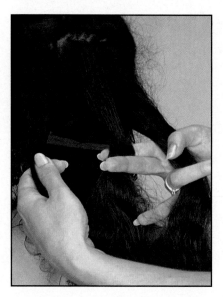

4. Continue underbraiding along the hair length for several inches, leaving an inch or two unbraided at the ends. Clip each strand individually to keep the strands in place.

5. Release the middle section of hair and divide it into three equal-size strands. The three strands of the top braid will be joined to these strands.

6. Lay the ends of the three strands from the top braid over the strands of the middle braid in preparation for joining them.

7. Pick up the three joined strands and continue underbraiding with them. Reach under the center strand to the right strand. Direct the right strand under the center and into the center position.

8. Then reach under the center strand to the left strand and bring it to the center position. Use tension and keep your hands close to the head as you braid the joined strands.

9. Repeat the underbraiding to within a few inches of the ends. Clip each strand individually as you did for the top braid.

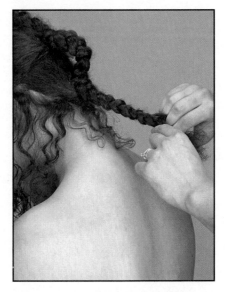

10. Divide the bottom section into three equal-size strands.

11. Join the ends of the middle braid with the three strands of the bottom section as in Steps 6 and 7. Underbraid this section to the ends.

12. Secure the end of the bottom braid and turn it under to form a loop. Secure the loop to the nape of the neck with a bobby pin. Complete the design by arranging the hair framing the face, curling it if necessary.

CAREER MOVES
TWO-STRAND OVERLAP

This is a smooth, understated design very suitable for business situations. It requires long hair at the sides. Strands are picked up from the hairline at both sides of the head, brought to the center back, and crossed over each other. A few large strands create a simple look; for a more intricate design, use more strands that are smaller. A draped effect can be achieved by leaving more slack in the hair before pinning the strands in place. In this design, the remaining hair is finished off with a three-strand underbraid.

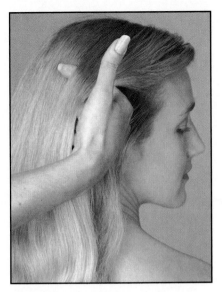

1. Comb the hair smooth and create a side part. Pick up a section from one side of the front hairline.

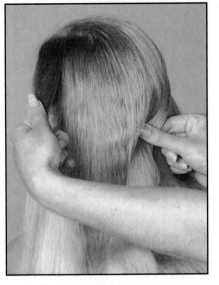

2. Direct the section to the center back. Select an equal amount of hair from the opposite side and direct it to the center back.

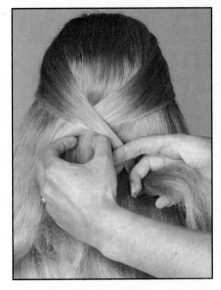

3. Cross the left strand over the right one and hold the two strands in position.

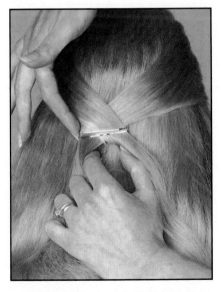

4. Secure the two strands by pinning a bobby pin across the overlap. Position a second bobby pin from the opposite side to ensure a firm hold.

5. Repeat the procedure, picking up, crossing and pinning with two new strands. Position the overlap of the two strands to cover the bobby pins holding the previous overlap.

6. Continue picking up and crossing down the center back until the last section has been picked up from the scalp.

(continued)

7. Temporarily pin this last crossing to hold it in place. The pins will be removed once the remaining hair is braided.

8. Divide the remaining hair into three equal-size strands. Underbraid by crossing each outside strand under the center strand, alternating from left to right.

9. Fasten the ends and remove the bobby pins from the last crossing.

10. For a casual look, this design can be worn with the braid hanging free.

11. To tuck the braid under, curve the end and roll the braid toward the scalp. Secure it underneath by attaching it to the nape of the neck with a bobby pin.

12. Only the two-strand overlap shows in the finished tucked-under version, producing a clean, uncluttered design.

SLEEK AND FESTIVE
TWO-STRAND OVERLAP AND FOUR-STRAND ROUND BRAID

In this glamorous design, each side is done in a two-strand overlap and the two sides are joined in a four-strand round braid. The four-strand round braid is an unusual braid variation that creates a distinctive chain pattern. Since there are four strands to control, this braid tends to be a little more difficult than a three-strand braid, but if you think about the path of the strands, it's not too hard. Outside strands travel under two strands and back over one. Once you become familiar with this round braid, you can experiment with it and position it anywhere.

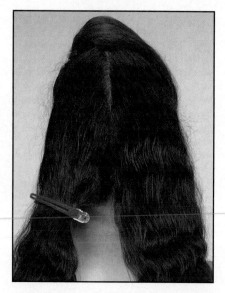

1. Section the front area from the back with a parting that extends across the top of the head from ear to ear. Clip the front area out of your way.

2. Part the remaining hair down the center back of the head. Clip one side to keep it out of the way while you work on the other side.

3. Pick up a triangular section of hair at the point where the two parts meet and divide it into two strands. Cross the right strand over the left.

4. Pick up additional hair from the scalp on the left side of the two strands.

5. Cross this picked-up section over to the right side of the crossed strands and join it with the strand in your right hand.

6. Pick up additional hair from the scalp on the right side.

7. Cross this picked-up section over and add it to the strand in your left hand.

8. Repeat this left-over-right and right-over-left overlap all the way down this side of the head.

9. Remember to run your hands down the lengths of hair to smooth and untangle the strands before overlapping them.

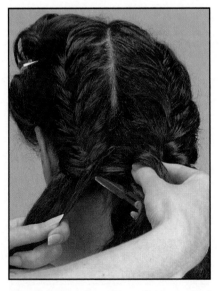

10. Continue until you have picked up all the hair on the first side. Clip the strands to hold them in place while you repeat the procedure on the other side.

11. You now have four strands—two from each side. You will use these strands to create a four-strand round braid. Begin by crossing the two center strands.

12. Grasp the outside left strand and direct it under the two center strands.

(continued)

13. Then direct that same strand back *over* the last strand it went under.

14. Now grasp the outside right strand and move it under the two center strands and back over the last strand it went under.

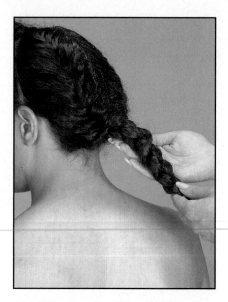

15. Continue braiding the four strands. Outside strands go *under* two and back *over* one. When you reach the ends, secure them with a coated band. Tuck the finished braid under and pin.

16. Release the top hair and brush it smoothly upward. Hold the ends and fold them under.

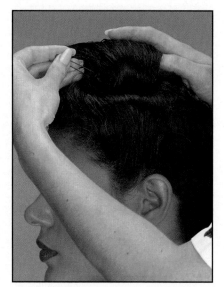

17. Roll the hair down toward the scalp and pin to secure the roll.

18. Make sure the size of the roll balances the total design. Adjust the size of the roll by tucking it tighter or expanding it.

HIGH SOCIETY
ROLL WITH FOUR-STRAND BRAID

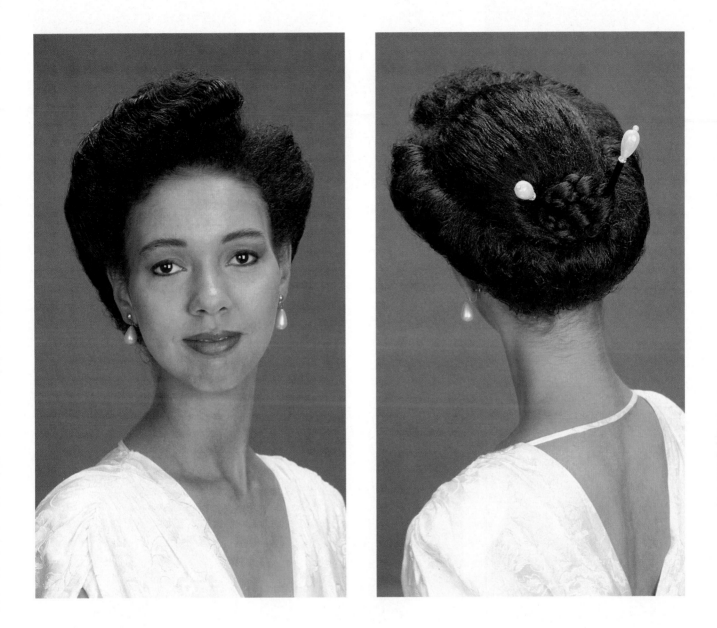

A curved roll around the edges of the hairline sets the foundation for this design. The roll is created by turning smaller segments of hair and pinning them into position to form a curved shape that follows the hairline. Turning the hair segments tightly will produce a smaller roll. An optional accent is the four-strand round braid from the crown of the head.

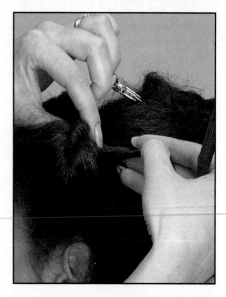

1. Section off the crown in a circular shape and pin it out of the way. Beginning on the side of the part with the least hair, separate a small section and comb the hair smooth.

2. Lightly twist the ends of the section so that they form a small strand.

3. Fold the section up and in toward the crown and adjust the height of the fold so that it is flattering. Tuck the twisted ends inside.

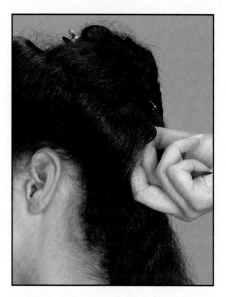

4. Secure the section with a bobby pin.

5. Separate the next small segment to continue the roll. The angle at which you hold the hair before you twist is important—check to make sure the new segment will blend with the ones already rolled.

6. Fold the ends of the new segment inside and blend the height to the one already created.

7. Insert hairpins to connect the two segments once the new one is in position.

8. When you have reached the center back, stop and move to the front. Separate a section of hair at the front right next to the first roll that you made.

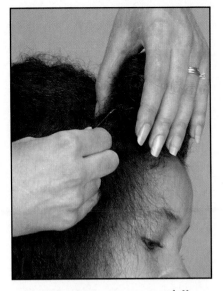

9. Roll the front section carefully to create the desired height. Pin the roll as before. Make sure the height and width of the rolls at the face are flattering. You can then work to blend in that balance with the roll at the back.

10. Work around toward the back, combing each section smooth before directing it upward.

11. When you position the final roll at the back, blend it to the rolls pinned previously. Check to make sure the entire roll is balanced before you proceed to the braid.

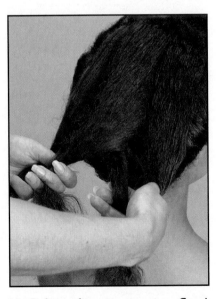

12. Release the crown section. Comb the hair back and divide it into four equal-size strands. Cross the two center strands.

(continued)

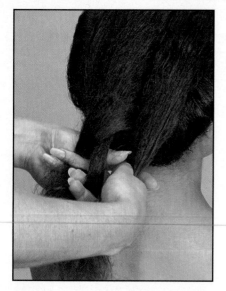

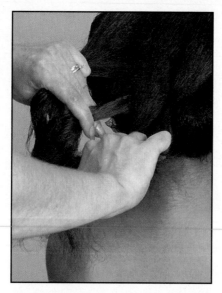

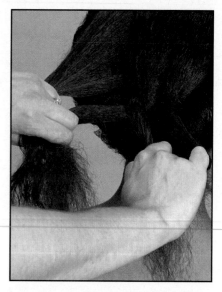

13. With your left hand, reach under to the outside right strand and grasp it.

14. Direct this strand under the two center strands.

15. Then direct the same strand over the last strand it went under. Repeat with the outside left strand, guiding it under the two center strands and over the last strand it went under.

16. Continue braiding the four strands. Outside strands go *under* two and back *over* one. When you reach the ends, secure them with a coated band.

17. Curve the finished braid into a small coil and position it above the rolls of hair.

18. Pin it into place, forming a braided accent to the rolls.

MODERN GLAMOUR
TWO-STRAND ROPE WITH FRENCH TWIST

The classic vertical roll, also known as a French twist, is combined with a two-strand rope in the front for a sophisticated design. To create the rope, two strands are individually twisted and then twisted together. New sections are picked up on either side and combined with the strands as the rope continues.

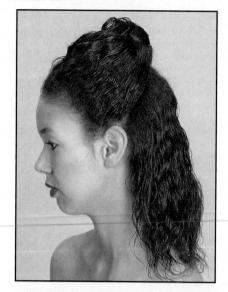

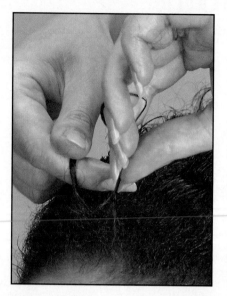

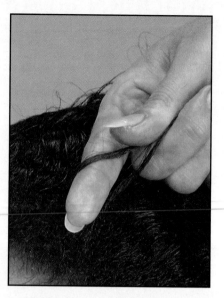

1. Begin this design by sectioning the front from the back. Here we used a diagonal sectioning line from behind the ear to the crown.

2. Secure the back lengths out of the way and section a triangle at the front hairline. Divide this section into two equal-size strands. Twist both strands clockwise close to the base of the strands at the scalp.

3. Holding your right hand palm up, insert your forefinger between the two strands.

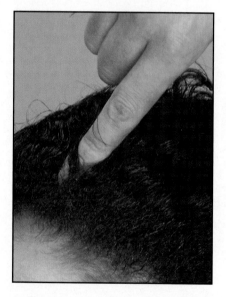

4. Turn your hand counterclockwise to position your palm down.

5. Pick up hair from the left side of the two strands and add it to the left-hand strand. Do the same on the right side.

6. Twist both of the enlarged strands clockwise, remembering to twist close to the scalp. With your palm up, insert your forefinger between the two twisted strands.

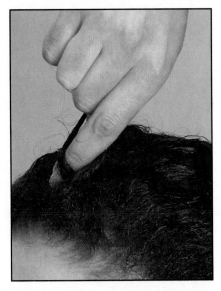

7. Turn your hand palm down to twist the two strands together.

8. Continue down the center of the head until all of the hair from the front has been picked up. Try to pick up equal amounts of hair when you add new sections to each strand. It is very important to maintain tension on each strand as you twist it clockwise.

9. Continue the two-strand rope down the length of the free strands. Hold both strands and twist them both at the same time. Your forefinger should position itself automatically between the strands. Then turn your hand over so the palm is down.

10. When you reach the ends of the strands, fasten the ends of the rope with a coated band.

11. Release the back hair lengths.

12. Place the rope out of the way and comb the remaining hair to one side, angling it slightly upward. Lay the tail end of a comb down the center back. The comb should be angled away from the head.

(continued)

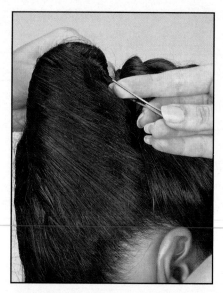

13. Wrap the free lengths around the tail of the comb. This will help you make a clean fold in the hair.

14. Remove the comb and twist the remaining ends in the same direction. Pull the twist upward and fan the twist to balance the vertical roll.

15. Curve the free ends down in a circle at the crown and pin to secure.

16. To hold the edge of the roll, insert hairpins along the rolled edge.

17. Wrap the free ends of the two-strand rope around the top of the twist and pin the ends to hold it in position.

18. You can add an ornament or hair swatch to balance the design, if you wish. Here a four-strand braided hair swatch is wrapped around the rope to increase the rope's size and texture.

ELEGANT SIMPLICITY
ASYMMETRICAL CLUSTER OF TWISTS

Single-strand twists give a texture completely different from two-strand twists and are very easy to do. Tightly twisting individual strands of hair will force the strands to coil and bend automatically. In this design, several coiled strands are pinned in a cluster on one side of the head, creating a contrast between the smooth pageboy hairstyle and this intriguing texture of twists. This is a free-form technique—the number and size of the twists can vary. Large sections create graphic patterns, and small sections create more delicate twists.

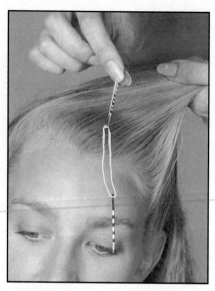

1. Separate a large section of hair at the front and comb it off to one side.

2. Make a fastener by attaching bobby pins to either end of an elastic band.

3. Secure the hair at the front in a ponytail by attaching one bobby pin to the base of the hair, winding the elastic band around the hair, and then attaching the other bobby pin.

4. Pick up a small strand of hair from the ponytail. Twist this strand several times.

5. Continue twisting the strand until the hair coils and bends automatically. Position the coil against the head so that it suits your design plan.

6. Secure the ends of the twist with a bobby pin. If the hair is very fine, you may need a small bobby pin. Secure the loop of the coils as well. If needed, apply gel to control stray ends.

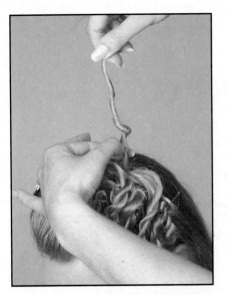

7. Continue to twist and curl the rest of the hair in the ponytail. Keep the size of your twists equal. Check to see that each twist fits in with the design before you pin the top and bottom.

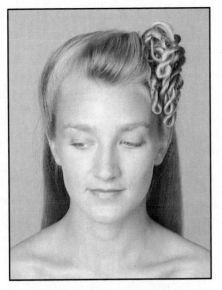

8. The finished twists should show a balanced design with no pins showing.

9. To achieve a shorter pageboy look with long hair, roll under several inches of the back hair at the nape. Begin by grasping the ends and folding them back over your hand.

10. Remove your hand and continue to roll the hair up toward the head.

11. Secure the roll by pinning it to the nape area.

12. Finish the pageboy by fanning the edges of the roll behind the ears. This technique offers the option of a shorter look without the permanence of a haircut.

SHEER FANTASY
SINGLE-STRAND TWIST CHIGNON

In this design, large individual strands are twisted and pinned in a free-form pattern at the nape. The shape of the chignon can be varied to create an elongated oval in the center back or a wide oval at the nape. Shorter hair lengths around the forehead can be left out to create softness.

This design can be created with your own hair, of course, but if your hair is too short you can use an added hairpiece, as we have done here. The first six steps show how to properly attach the hairpiece. The remaining steps show how to create the hairstyle.

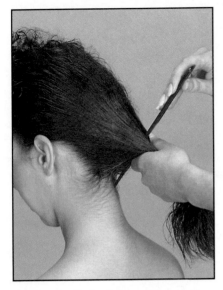

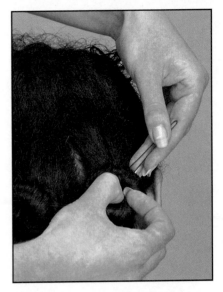

1. Comb all the hair to the center back and divide the hair in half down the middle. A tail comb can help do this quickly.

2. Create two ponytails and secure them with coated bands at the nape.

3. Twist one ponytail and wrap it around its base in a coil. Pin it in place. Repeat with the other ponytail.

4. This hairpiece is attached to two combs that interlock when closed.

5. Open the hairpiece and place it over the coiled ponytails.

6. Close the comb around the coiled ponytails and snap the ends together.

(continued)

7. Next create the free-form twists. Select a strand from the hairpiece and twist the strand several times.

8. Continue twisting until the hair coils and folds. Secure the twist with pins. Work around the perimeter of the hairpiece toward the center.

9. Create additional twists and secure them with pins.

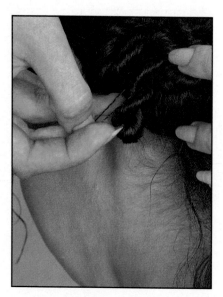

10. Continue twisting, being sure to adjust the position of each twist to create a well-balanced design.

11. Pin each twist at the top and bottom to hold it in position.

12. If you leave some of the hairpiece dangling down, the twisted area forms a chignon that acts as a transition between the natural hair and the hairpiece. You can also create twists with the entire hairpiece, giving the hair a more formal look.

SPIRITED TEXTURE
PROJECTED UNDERBRAID WITH CENTER PART

This style is a good choice either for a young girl or as an active style for a young woman. The two sides are underbraided, and the two underbraids are joined at the center back to produce a large underbraid that hangs free. The underbraids project from the head, creating an interesting graphic design.

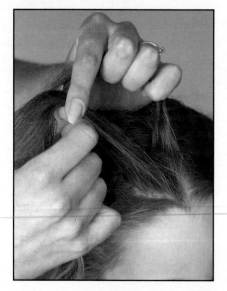

1. Begin by parting the hair down the center and combing each side smooth. Select a triangular section of hair from the front of one side and divide it into three equal-size strands.

2. Reach under and grasp the left strand.

3. Cross the left strand under the center strand so that the left strand is now in the center position.

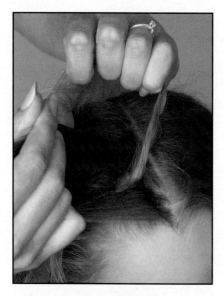

4. Reach under to grasp the right strand. Cross the right strand under the center strand so that the right strand is now in the center position.

5. Continue underbraiding, but pick up and add new sections of hair to each outside strand as you go along. Pick up new sections of hair from the area between the hairline and the braid and add them to the left strand; pick up new sections from the area between the center part and the braid and add them to the right strand.

6. As each new, combined strand is formed, reach under the center strand and cross the new strand under it.

7. As you work toward the back of the head, keep the braid parallel to the center part.

8. When you reach the center back of the head, secure each strand of the braid with clips.

9. Underbraid the other side in the same way, making sure that the positions of the two braids match.

10. When both braids reach the center back, they will be joined together into one braid.

11. Join the center and left strand of the left braid in your left hand and separate the right strand.

12. This right strand of the left braid combines with the left strand of the right braid to create a second strand.

(continued)

13. The third strand is created by combining the center and right strand of the right braid.

14. Begin to underbraid with the three newly formed strands.

15. As you braid, pick up new sections of hair from either side of the braid and add them to each outside strand.

16. When all of the hair has been picked up from the scalp and added to the strands, underbraid the remaining loose hair.

17. Continue to underbraid to the ends.

18. Secure the ends with a coated elastic band. A barrette or other ornament can be used to cover the elastic band.

TOP TWIST
SINGLE-STRAND TWISTS

Large twists are fun alternatives to ponytails and a great way to design wet longer hair when something simple and quick is in order. Three twists are placed on top of the head, and each twist is ornamented with a bow tied around its base. Consider this design for a girl straight from the bath or out of the pool. Tip: Conditioner can be applied to the hair first, giving the hair protection against fun in the sun.

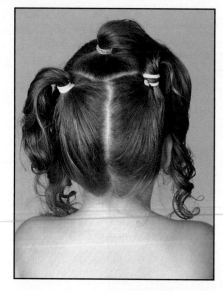

1. Begin by creating three ponytails. Gather the front hair into one ponytail on top of the head. Then divide the back hair in half and create two ponytails behind the center one.

2. Start twisting one of the ponytails. Continue to twist in the same direction until the strand begins to coil and bend over automatically.

3. Hold the twisted shape in position. Bring the free end down and wrap it around the base of the twist.

4. Insert a hairpin into the base to secure the end.

5. Repeat Steps 2 through 4 on the other two ponytails.

6. Each twist will take on a character of its own. You can make them stand upright or allow them to fold over. Ribbon can be tied around the base of each twist to dress up the design.

CASUAL GRACE
INVERTED OVERBRAID

This design is frequently called a French braid. It uses a variation of the basic overbraiding technique in which new sections of hair are gathered and added to the outside strands as you braid. The outside strands become larger as the braiding continues. The resulting pattern is an inverted braid that lies flat to the head. A centered braid is common, but that is only one of the many styles you can create with this technique.

1. Comb the hair smooth and then separate a triangular section at the front hairline. Divide this section into three strands. Grasp the left strand with your thumb and forefinger and cross it over the center strand so that it is now in the center position.

2. Use your thumb and forefinger to grasp the right strand and cross it over the center strand.

3. Release the left strand onto the hair below. Pick up a new section of hair at the left side from the area between the hairline and the braid. Pick up the strand you dropped along with this new strand.

4. Cross this new, combined strand over the center strand, keeping all the strands taut.

5. Transfer the center strand of hair to your other hand, still keeping all three strands separate. Release the right strand onto the hair below. Pick up a new section of hair from the area between the hairline and the braid. Pick up the strand you dropped along with this new strand.

6. Hold the strands as shown so you can reach across the center to grasp the new, combined strand on the right.

7. Cross this combined strand over the center strand. To keep the braid flat, maintain consistent tension and work close to the head. Keep the hair smooth by running your hand down the strands as you go along.

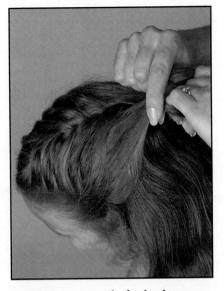

8. When you reach the back, you no longer need to drop the strand to be combined with the picked-up section. Hold all three strands in one hand and pick up the new section with the thumb and forefinger of your other hand. Direct the picked-up section upward to join the outside strand.

9. Once you have picked up all the hair, continue overbraiding the three loose strands. Cross the right strand over the center strand.

10. Next, cross the left strand over the center strand.

11. Continue the overbraiding technique to the ends of the strands.

12. Secure the ends with ribbon or decorative holders if desired.

YOUNG SPIRIT
ASYMMETRICAL TWO-STRAND ROPE

The two-strand rope is not a true braid, since it involves only two strands, but it produces an interesting twisted pattern that is an attractive alternative to braids. Each strand is twisted independently, and the two strands are then twisted together. The resulting texture resembles a rope. When you combine this technique with sections picked up from the scalp, the rope sits on top of the hair the way a projected braid does. The design used here features an asymmetrical rope moving along the front hairline from one side to the other. The hair at the back is left free and can be set with hot rollers for additional curl.

1. Part the hair to separate the front area from the back. Comb the front hair to one side.

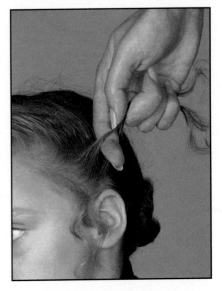

2. Take a rectangular section of hair and divide it into two equal-size strands. Twist each strand clockwise simultaneously. Twist only near the base, keeping your fingers close to the scalp.

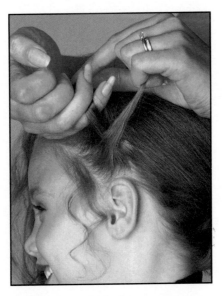

3. Holding your hand palm up, insert your forefinger between the two strands.

4. Turn your wrist over so your palm is facing down. This automatically twists the two strands together.

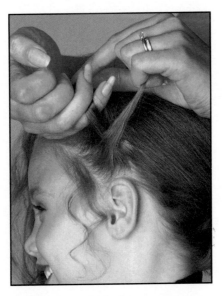

5. Using your little finger, part completely across the front section to pick up a new section.

6. Combine the new section with the strand toward the face and twist the combined strand clockwise.

(continued)

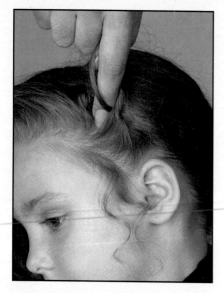

7. Once again, turn your hand palm upward and place your forefinger between the two strands. Turn your hand palm down to twist the two strands together.

8. Continue creating the rope across the top of the head, adding new sections of hair as you go along.

9. Try to keep the size of the picked-up sections equal. This will create an even pattern.

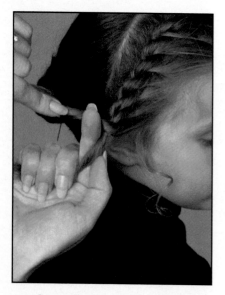

10. Once all the sections of hair have been picked up and incorporated into the rope, continue creating the rope with the remaining loose hair. A turn of the wrist will automatically twist the two strands together.

11. When the rope is finished, secure the ends with a coated band.

12. If you want additional curl in the back hair, use a curling iron or spiral hot rollers.

INGENUE
HALO OVERBRAID

This braid is perfect for a special occasion in a girl's life. A few loose tendrils soften the area around the face, and you can incorporate dried flowers to customize the design by repeating wardrobe colors.

An important step in this design is even distribution of the hair around the curve of the head prior to beginning the braid. The basic technique used here is overbraiding with hair picked up and added to the outside strands before they cross over the center strand. This design can also be done on wet hair, which creates a more casual finish that lies closer to the head.

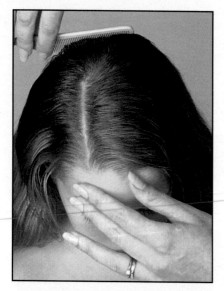

1. Choose the location of the braid. The location will determine how you distribute the hair. For this design, the hair was distributed off a short side part. Mist the hair lightly with water to control the hair before braiding.

2. Section a triangular area on the side of the part with the most hair. Subdivide it into three equal-size strands. Cross the right strand over the center strand so that the right strand is now in the center position.

3. Grasp the left strand and cross it over the center strand so that the left strand moves into the center position. Keep your hands close to the head.

4. Release the right strand into the hair below. Pick up a new section of hair from the area between the hairline and the braid. Pick up the dropped strand with this new section.

5. Drape the new section on your thumb. Run your hand down the length of the hair to clear the strand from the hair below.

6. Transfer the center strand and the new strand to the opposite hand. Grasp the new, combined strand with your thumb and forefinger.

7. Cross the new strand over the center strand.

8. Now release the strand on the left into the hair below. Use your thumb to pick up a new section of hair from the area between the part and the braid. Pick up the dropped strand with the new section.

9. Cross this new strand over the center strand, and tighten up any slack in the strands.

10. Continue around the curve of the head, trying to pick up equal amounts of hair each time and maintaining symmetry. Mist the hair with water periodically to control stray strands. This is especially helpful if the hair is wavy.

11. Direct the braid so that it curves around the back of the head. As you round the back, include all of the hair from the nape of the neck in the picked-up sections.

12. To pivot the pattern of picked-up sections around the end of the part, section triangular areas radiating from the end of the part.

(continued)

13. Continue overbraiding on the other side, keeping the braid high and balanced with the first side. Remember to keep your hands close to the head to maintain tension.

14. Continue the curve to form a braided circle on the top of the head.

15. Once you have picked up all of the hair from the scalp, continue to overbraid the remaining loose hair.

16. Secure the ends with a coated elastic band and coil the free part of the braid into a tight circle.

17. Pin the braid into position with hairpins.

18. An optional step is to release a few strands near the hairline to soften the line around the face. If you wish, you can curl the strands with a curling iron.